I Love Bugs

By Steve Parker
Illustrated by Richard Draper

First published in 2006 by
Miles Kelly Publishing Ltd
Bardfield Centre, Great Bardfield, Essex, CM7 4SL

Copyright © Miles Kelly Publishing Ltd 2006

2 4 6 8 10 9 7 5 3 1

Editorial Director Belinda Gallagher
Art Director Jo Brewer
Junior Designer Candice Bekir
Cover Artworker Stephan Davis
Production Manager Elizabeth Brunwin
Reprographics Stephan Davis

ISBN 1-84236-780-3

Printed in China

British Library Cataloguing-in-Publication Data
A catalogue record for this book is available
from the British Library

www.mileskelly.net
info@mileskelly.net

Contents

Dragonfly

Dragonflies are fierce hunting insects. They have big eyes that take up over half of their head, and a sharp mouth for cutting up their meals. They hunt smaller insects, such as flies, around rivers, lakes and ponds.

Water baby

A young dragonfly is called a nymph. It doesn't have any wings. It lives in a pond and is a fierce hunter, just like adult dragonflies.

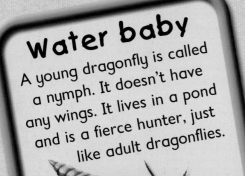

The wings make a whirring noise as they beat up and down ten times every second.

When it has found a meal, the dragonfly begins to bite it into pieces to eat the softer parts.

The dragonfly's eye is made of many tiny parts. Each part can see a small area of the view.

Dragonflies catch their food with their legs. They hold out the front legs like a basket to scoop up flies, gnats and moths.

Honey bee

Honey bees live in a group, or colony, in a nest. They share jobs such as finding food, cleaning the nest and caring for young. In fact, they will even die for each other so that the whole colony can survive.

Some holes in the nest contain food the bees have made from flower nectar and pollen – this is honey.

Flower power!

As bees collect pollen, they spread it from flower to flower, to make new seeds. If there were fewer bees, there would be fewer flowers.

A bee's sting is at the end of its body. If it stings an enemy, the back part of the body is torn off, and the bee dies.

A bees' nest has hundreds of six-sided holes with wax walls. Here, young bees hatch into grubs.

Praying mantis

Few insects are fiercer than the praying mantis. It is named because its front legs are folded, as if it is praying. It waits for a fly or moth to come near, then it snaps it up with its sharp legs.

The mantis has big eyes and hunts mainly by sight. Sometimes it creeps up on its prey, but it usually grabs its meal out of mid air.

The front legs have sharp spines that stick into the meal. The mantis chops and tears up its food.

The mantis is green to match the leaves around it. This means that its prey does not notice any danger until it is too late.

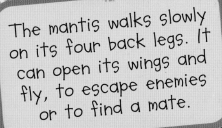

The mantis walks slowly on its four back legs. It can open its wings and fly, to escape enemies or to find a mate.

Monarch butterfly

No insect flies further than the monarch butterfly. Each year these big butterflies fly hundreds of kilometres on their long journeys, called migrations. They do this to breed, and then they die.

Full circle

Butterflies lay eggs, which hatch into caterpillars, which become chrysalises, which ... become butterflies!

The monarch's wings are 10 centimetres across. The bright patterns and spots warn enemies that this butterfly isn't good to eat.

There are long feelers on the butterfly's head. These can 'smell' the air for scents of flowers.

The butterfly's tongue is shaped like a curled-up drinking straw. It unrolls to drink flower juices.

Monarch butterflies can fly an amazing 150 kilometres in a single day.

Earwig

Earwigs don't crawl into people's ears. They like dark, damp places such as under tree bark, logs and stones. During the day they like to hide. At night they come out to feed on flower petals, one of their favourite foods.

The pincers are used to fold up the wings after flying. The female earwig has almost straight pincers. This is a male earwig. His pincers are curved.

Caring mum

A mother earwig takes good care of her eggs. She cleans and protects them.

Earwigs have a low, flat body. They can crawl into a narrow opening to hide from enemies, such as spiders, frogs and birds.

The two flat parts on the earwig's back are its wing covers. Beneath these are two large wings.

Army ants

Army ants march in long lines across the forest floor until they feel hungry. Then they stop. Some begin to make a nest that will last for a few days. Others set out to find food. They kill any animal they come across.

The ants crowd around a victim. They bite and sting it, then chop it into tiny pieces with their strong 'jaws'.

There can be thousands and thousands of ants in one group.

Giant queen
Only a queen ant lays eggs. She is huge — five times bigger than a guard, which is twice as big as a worker.

Some ants go off in smaller groups to search for more food.

Locusts

Locusts are a type of grasshopper. They live in hot, dry areas. Sometimes, when lots of rain falls and plants grow quickly, locusts feed well. Then more locusts are born. Soon there are millions of them, and they take to the air in a huge, hungry cloud.

As locusts feed, they crawl or hop from plant to plant. They use their long, strong back legs to leap away from danger.

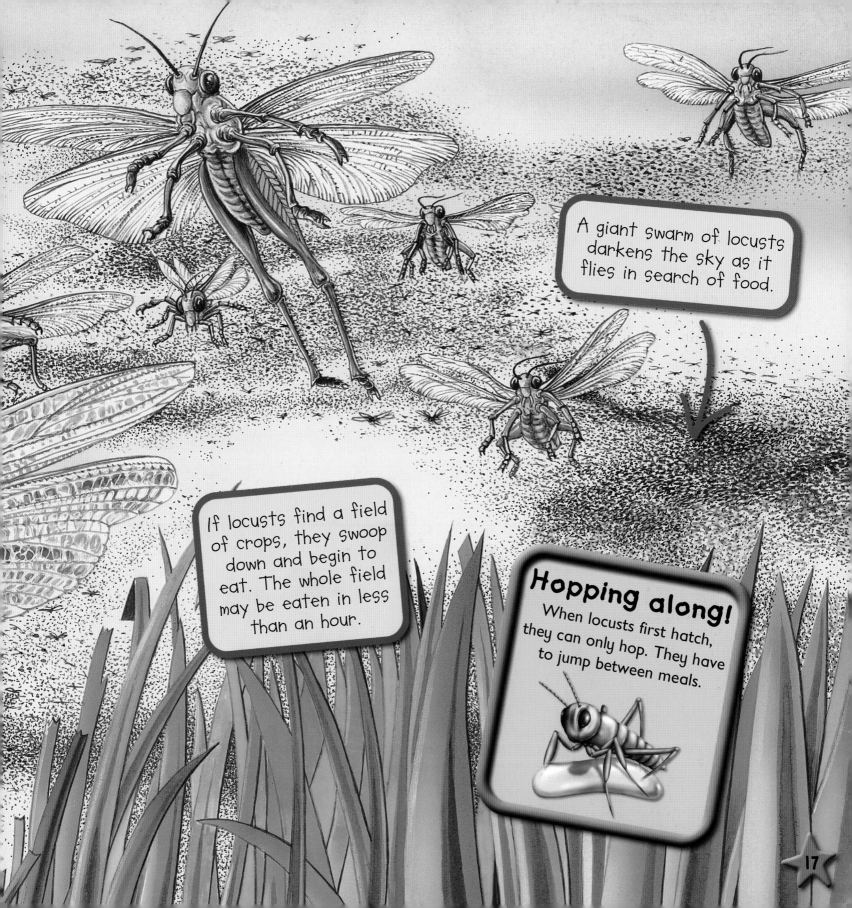

A giant swarm of locusts darkens the sky as it flies in search of food.

If locusts find a field of crops, they swoop down and begin to eat. The whole field may be eaten in less than an hour.

Hopping along!
When locusts first hatch, they can only hop. They have to jump between meals.

Great diving beetle

The great diving beetle lives in ponds. It is fast and fierce, with big, sharp jaws to grab and eat animals such as tadpoles, worms and baby fish. The beetle traps bubbles of air at the water's surface. It stores the air under its wings so it can breathe underwater.

The beetle hunts using its big eyes. Its antennae (feelers) sense ripples in the water made by small animals.

The beetle grabs its dinner, such as this tadpole, with its front feet then pulls it into its sharp jaws.

This is a female great diving beetle – she has grooves, or furrows, along her back. The male's back is smooth and shiny.

The strong legs work like paddles to row through the water.

A tasty meal
Diving beetles quickly catch food that falls into the pond – from flies to worms.

Moon moth

The moon moth flies like a ghost through the night sky. Most moths like the light of the moon as they search for plant juices to drink. By day they rest in cracks in rocks or among leaves. Butterflies prefer to fly during the day.

Moths have feelers shaped like feathers.

The wide wings have large spots, like staring eyes. These make the moth look like a big-eyed owl, which scares away enemies.

The moon moth's long tail is mainly for show, to attract a partner. By day, as the moth rests, the tail looks like old, curled-up leaves.

Make a moth

Fold some paper in half. Open it up and paint moth wings on one side. Fold the paper and press down. Open it to see all the moth!

Mosquito

Many insects spread germs and disease. The mosquito is one of the most dangerous. In hotter parts of the world, when it bites people to suck their blood, it may pass on a terrible illness such as malaria or yellow fever.

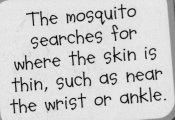

The mosquito searches for where the skin is thin, such as near the wrist or ankle.

A long, sharp feeding tube is stuck into the skin to suck up blood.

As the mosquito sucks blood, its body swells up like a red balloon. Then it slides out its feeding tube and buzzes off.

Growing up

Baby mosquitoes, or nymphs, grow up in ponds and ditches. They don't look like their parents to begin with.

Fun facts

Dragonfly These insects are not really flies, and they are called 'dragonflies' because of their fierce jaws.

Honey bee A worker honey bee usually lives for just 28 to 35 days.

Praying mantis This insect is able to turn its head round in all directions.

Monarch butterfly If it rains, the monarch butterfly cannot fly.

Earwig Some earwigs have been known to tunnel up to 20 metres into the soil.

Army ants There are about 150 different kinds of army ant.

Locusts A swarm of locusts has been known to travel 5000 kilometres in ten days.

Great diving beetle The young (larvae) of the great diving beetle may be even bigger and fiercer than the adults.

Moon moth These moths do not have mouths and cannot feed – they live for just one week.

Mosquito The wings of the mosquito beat 500 times each second.